SOCRATES IS MORTAL

Stephen
Williams

DOS MADRES

2025

DOS MADRES PRESS INC.

P.O. Box 294, Loveland, Ohio 45140
www.dosmadres.com   editor@dosmadres.com

Dos Madres is dedicated to the belief that the small press is essential to the vitality of contemporary literature as a carrier of the new voice, as well as the older, sometimes forgotten voices of the past. And in an ever more virtual world, to the creation of fine books pleasing to the eye and hand.

Dos Madres is named in honor of Vera Murphy and Libbie Hughes, the "Dos Madres" whose contributions have made this press possible.

Dos Madres Press, Inc. is an Ohio Not For Profit Corporation and a 501 (c) (3) qualified public charity. Contributions are tax deductible.

Executive Editor: Robert J. Murphy

Illustration & Book Design: Elizabeth H. Murphy
www.illusionstudios.net

Typeset in Adobe Garamond Pro & Garamond
ISBN 978-1-962847-40-7
Library of Congress Control Number: 2025949567

CONTENTS

◆ PHOSPHORESCENT FICTION ◆

◆ CLICK ◆

◆

SOCRATES IS MORTAL

◆

All men are mortal.
Socrates is a man.
Therefore Socrates is mortal.

—An example of a syllogism
commonly used in Renaissance textbooks

◆ DEAD END / AD INFINITUM ◆

There's a knock
at the heart of things.
Will you answer?

The earliest naturalists revealed
were revealed by the god Mercury

Chemical beings dying bright metallic blue

Those aspects that resisted interpretation were considered *decorative*, while those too charged with meaning were labeled *ornamental*.

—Roberto Calasso, *Tiepolo Pink*

The void was too full of meaning
so it ornamented itself
with the world.

The dark was too full of meaning
so it ornamented itself
with light.

Fate was too full of meaning
so it ornamented itself
with chance.

History was too full of meaning
so it ornamented itself
with apocalypse.

God was too full of meaning
so he ornamented himself
with humankind.

And humankind, cracked cup,
can never fill with meaning—
they live and die instead.

A LIFE

'craftsman of the snowflake'
so Berryman, so much
convulsed, called God—

whose suffering was undignified,
who would have died
for his art, but instead
a waste of shame succumbed quite simply
the only way he knew how

did he avert his gaze
with an upward look?
—who knew damnation is real
and very close
and runs through everything like the Mississippi

converted himself in 1970 toward a god he could almost
dare to love
emptied his tin cup heart
scoured it clean

then?

o from out of the tar and ash and shit
from the origin pit

'accept my amazement'

O COLD THREAD OF SPIRIT

with the nerves twinkling upon it

what sustains you?

little flagellum, tail
attached to no body, frail

life,
too frail perhaps for Life to deign to crush

what small secret
thing, thus
shields you from annihilation?

The nerves and their intelligence
miracle of the small
beady, pearlescent
in my imagination of it

The fractal scaffold
its infinite crystal steps
up the nerves
and up the mind

toward a distant god

who made the damned thing in the first place
wild but not random
whose presence
amazement demands

a neural Babel
eminently shatterable
and it flashes as it shatters

God that is nothing
trying to be God,

into the depth of your attempt,
admit me.

POEM

Things of this world
come together,
fall apart.

Only dust is immortal.

THE LIGHT AT THE END OF THE TUNNEL

All of life takes place at the end of an infinitely long
tunnel exactly the shape and size of the human eye.

But if the tunnel is infinitely long, why is the light not
infinitely small?

Pumice is rough
so we use it
to make things smooth.

Catullus, for instance,
used it
to polish his book.

Words are false
so we use them
to make things true.

True like an orange.

THE PRODUCTIONS OF TIME

terrify me.

In spring, Alan Turing
wore a gas mask
to help his allergies.

All the ants on earth
weigh more than all the people.

Rasputin's daughter
moved to America
and became a lion tamer.

Piero della Francesca died
the same day Columbus landed
in the New World.

Killing a snake
is the same
as having a snake.

Joan Didion said that.

AFTER SIMONIDES

God is an aristocrat.

Why did God disguise himself
as a virus
when the world is already sick?

Because the world is sick,
it makes a good disguise.

Why did God disguise himself
as three crows on a wire
while the world burns?

To escape the flames.

Why did God disguise himself
as a cough?

So he could fit inside a human body.

Why did God disguise himself
as a mushroom
when the world is full of poison?

In solidarity with the mushroom.

Why did God disguise himself
as law?

Because his best-known attribute is grace.

Why did God disguise himself
in the first place?

The commentaries disagree.

Either to make himself
comprehensible to his creatures,
or because he was afraid they would kill him.

THIS MORNING

The storm is gone.

In its place is peace
in the shape of a storm.

The whole pyramid reaches upward toward a single point.

A point is 'that which has no part.' Is nothing.

So the pyramid has no top. It really does go all the way to heaven.

Interesting to think about how
the point everything culminates in
might be you!

There, at the end of everything, the nothing there might be you!

THE END

Beautiful fish fan the warship's rusted, coral-crusted hulk.

I and my companions suffer
Cortés told Montezuma's
messenger

from a disease of the heart
only gold can cure

THE FLOWER

The flower takes
the form of a cry.
The flower aches:
it cannot be
other than it is.

Out to the edges
of its petals it
did not choose
what to be; down
to its roots it
did not choose
to be. The flower

has no inside or outside.
It contains
about a mouthful
of silence

in the form
of a cry. The cry
is the flower's,
is mine, is
the flower's,
is mine.

The flower
is the world.
Look! The flower!

TONGUES

We went ad fontes
and found a long tongue
sticking out of the earth
where the spring was supposed to be.

—

Salt was a dissolving star
on your tongue.

You swallowed
nothing.

—

The ox is on my tongue.

No: it's the sphinx.

—

My leather
tongue salt
words cured

—

There's a scratch on the sun.
There's a leaf on my tongue.

In the middle of the continent,

God's laughter zigzags among myrtle,

the garden sweats resin, the wild sugars run.

——

Since they cut my tongue out,
I move my throat
in mute shapes
to curse it.

Walk at dusk
window open
on an empty room

A curtain
turns over,
someone's voice

A broken heart does almost everything an intact heart does.

Don't you agree?

THINGS PEOPLE SAY

It's chaos. Or a tapestry.
Nothing happens to me.

Button your source.
Up to you of course.

Give me your coat.
The heart is a boat.

You're high on speed.
The heart is birdseed.

It's the spirit of the age.
Puts the cats in a rage.

I'll watch it just to see.
Somebody didn't tell me.

Open mouth filled with snow.
Quite so. Quite so. Now you know.

That I can't say.
And walked away.

Magnolias. May. Everything
will be good today.

◆ DON'T MOVE ◆

Did you lose your heart in nature?
No, I didn't, not there.

—Alfred Döblin, *Berlin Alexanderplatz*

The town is dark,
and the people in it,
and you going in among them.

THE SOUND THROUGH

The sound through sifts his life through
sleep as if sleep were a personal thing.
The sound through sinks down through
shadow-strata of sleep Hypnos tipped
a little at a time from a crystal decanter.
Deep in the night the sound through
sings in his sleep the song of the inner
surface of himself. A human croon, but
barely. Deep in himself, at the bottom
of the long vessel the night is the sound
through sings the liquid menace of his
sleep. It is the speed of the song coursing
through him. Preying on him. And then
it stops. Fades from black to black. Dissolves
into dream: which is a personal thing:
a dream dreamt by matter, by sound
dispersing and converging on a center:
hive it makes in its changes, secret path

Death and life combine to make life.

ONEIRIANA

Close your eyes, dark travels across dark.

Chunks of feldspar float
like icebergs in the Sea of Rains'
lava plain. The Superintendent
for the Dead and Missing
shipwrecked in the Mekong Delta.

A great silence swept over the labyrinth.

———

The narrator is a character
of a peculiar kind, writes Philip Pullman,
a disembodied consciousness
that flits, or swims, or alights
in the minds of the characters—
penetrates them perhaps
through the ear, perhaps
through the eye's pinhole.

———

Camões was jailed
for stealing from the dead.

———

The fascination of the story,
wash of past and future
on the dissolving face of the present.

—

Perhaps what you were
was hidden in the tamarisk
in a Phoenician palace
all this time, perhaps
deep in the folds of your brain.
But you are the one who must
put the person back together.

POWERS OF THE EARTH

At the Duncan conference, suddenly
I caught myself speaking
of metamorphosis, how it happens
despite itself, how the body in its
moment of excess, turns against itself

Imagine turning into a tree. It will break all your bones

So my brain slowly made new songlines in the earth and sky
of my mind, 'set free but with no bearings yet'—
so my body ripped up the old tracks, which were not false, which
were real, and true. I translated Catullus
white knuckled in the place I rode my nerves
and my nerves surging took me, the language like leather
my amputee teeth clenched. Outside the thaw sang, and my nerves
dissonantly joined.

—

A sequence of tones,
The give and take
Of emphasis, the wind's
Give and take.

You remember things—
You different person.
No slant or tint
To the mind's light,
Things rise from life
To meet your memory

Of them. Sweat rises
To your neck and brow.

The short line
Summons
Out of silence,
Signs. One
Sign.

—

The broken alphabets, the desiccated,
it is your lot to reassemble.
Out of hell and into history, Aeneas.
Shadowed unto us, omen-shapes across
unimaginable distances touch our ken
and, having charmed or instructed
or hurt us
in our inwardness, drift back into metaphysics
stained by wonder, stamped
with a human breath that says *These*

are the powers of the earth

Watch them rise in the wild dry air

Death has never heard of life
as he goes about his life
seeking pleasure, salving pain,
sweeping the floor.

The phoenix rose and took flight. Immediately the site was cordoned off and a white PVC tent set up over the heap of ashes so that none would blow away. After photographing the ashes—perhaps there was a pattern to their distribution, white and flaky here, dark and scaly there—the scientists began collecting samples. The government wanted to extract the knowledge the ash contained.

TACERE

English has no such word.

You can fall silent.

You can keep it to yourself.

You can shut the fuck up.

You can shush.

You can zip it.

TO ZERO

Whitehead called you
the most civilized of numbers,
disdaining the everyday trade
in sheep and grain.

Serene, aristocratic,
skipping to the front of the line
on my keyboard—
you are of that class
to whom the rules do not apply.

Joker in the deck
of quantity, zero
the unforgiving,
zero the ahistorical,
the ouroboral,
wicked little black halo—

pure abstraction
we invented
and leapt through.

TO THE ATOM

Adam gave names
to everything in nature
he could see.

But you, invisible atom—
you are named
for what you are not.

Indivisible
term the world
requires: if
all were endlessly
divisible, there would be
an infinite number
of things; the
world would
choke on dust . . .

Logical conclusion
of presocratic speculation
that turned out to be real!

That less than which
nothing can
be.

Little planet.
Little Saturn
with your crazy rings.

Sentinel guarding being,
who keeps the gate,
who keeps unbeing
at bay.

CLINAMEN

Mechanized free
will makes no sense,

but the will
unchecked
is monstrous.

Lucretius knew:
he lived
in a lurid world—

the sacred had fled the old gods
and had not yet taken hold
of the new;

it sat suspended,
unformed, in the interval.

It filled it like a gas.

BEGINNING WITH A QUESTION FROM RYSZARD KRYNICKI

So you want to exist,
little line? So you want to

be?

Be still, little line,
primordial mark,

be still.

Don't jag
or hook or curl
into shape.

Don't whirl
suddenly into words.

Don't move.

HELLO, FREEDOM MAN!

The first stanza adapts Ronald Reagan's
Farewell Address to the Nation, January 11, 1989.

A small story about a big ship, a refugee
and a sailor: one day the crew on the carrier *Midway*
spied on the horizon a leaky little boat.
In it were refugees hoping to get to America,
and as they approached the carrier, one cried out:
"Hello, American sailor. Hello, Freedom Man!"

Another story: Apollo, kaleidoscoping dolphin, man
and god, swam up alongside a ship—not refugees,
but merchants. Strange it was, but none cried out,
but they changed their course, and made their way
dreamlike toward Krisa. There's something very American
about this. And in their piety they took apart their boat

and built a temple that looked like a boat.
Through time they rebuilt it: daimones with human
faces graced the pediment—American
as The Luxor! or Graceland. But all are refugees
or emigrants from this place, the omphalos, the way
into the world and back out. All babies crying out

cry here. Tickle its navel and the world itself cries out.
This underlies the claim that we're all in the same boat,
to use the common expression. But each of us, midway
on our life's journey, feels it taking hold: the human
condition is too gentle a term. We refugees
from the amniotic bath became American,

and there is nothing more American
than to see a whale and cry out,
and galvanize the crew of misfits and refugees,
and weaponize the boat.
Only a few hundred human
generations. Only one way,

for Odysseus, home. Driving down the Eisenhower Expressway
past where it turns into the Reagan, past the Mall of America.
Scare quotes? Dead ground. There is nothing more human
than hypocrisy. No other animal is capable of it. Doesn't language
    itself cry out
for someone to save it? We are on a giant pleasure boat;
no one's taking any more refugees.

No way to go then. Who cried out?
America you should be buried in a boat,
with your gold, and something human for the refugees.

Water's ghost
is a current
with no water

Fire's ghost
is a flame
without fire

Air's ghost
is a gust
that suffocates

Earth's ghost
is a scattering
and a turning over
of nothing

Man's ghost is pure intellect

GODLIKE

Dissolve the seeds of things as
salt in an ocean of time.

Let your mind bound like horses in
vast grasslands of time.

Be as one who slipped
through the hands of time,

native of the primordial
infinite, or the end of time.

As a dream comes, unbidden,
forthright, at the right time,

seeks us each alone,
thrills and stills time,

with so light a touch as that make
in yourself of your time

a daemon-dwelling, before you withdraw
deep into your time.

EUROPE'S EAR

Hyacinth

A moan
bloomed.

Black Forest

The witch's fingers
take root
in European dirt.

A Dream

Instead of a liver I have diamonds.
When I twist my torso I feel them scrape and grind.

Anaxagoras said

the descent into hell
is the same
from every place.

Then he threw a dart at the map.

Dresden it is!

Jealous God

Your gaze torments
every flower.

AFTER TACITUS

They have a grove they call
the center of the world,
navel of the race;

no one enters
save in chains.

There they practice
human sacrifice.

It seems to work!

They control
vast tracts in the north.

Then Venus commanded Psyche to remake the mound of seeds the ants had finished sorting only moments before. Wheat barley millet bean lentil poppyseed vetch—a little heap of each—which to start with? And which to follow? In a puff of sexy perfume Venus vanished; the ants had already returned to their ant farm.

To remake the heap exactly as it was would yield the least random arrangement possible: its every data point would correspond to the original heap. To arrange it at random because one was ordered to do so would be the least random act possible because act would echo intention would echo command. And Venus' command was arbitrary, not random; it was cruel.

Psyche didn't want to obey and didn't.

Time passed. Psyche picked up a grain of millet between her thumb and forefinger. Fecund little pebble. She held it up to the light. She held it close to her eyes. She placed it back in the millet heap.

But I can't put the seed back in the same place on the little mound, she thought, because the relationships between the remaining seeds all changed, minutely it is true, when I took up the one seed.

How mysterious, the seven little mounds, fluid but unchanging. Like Heraclitan lakes.

Psyche skipped the remaining three tasks and became a poet.

for Andrew Joron

ON FIRE

The fire adjusts itself in the hearth,
holds up a few handfuls of light.

—

The gods sip ambrosia,
but fire lives on pure air.

—

s i g n
i g n i s
s i g n
i g n i s
s i g n
i g n i s
s i g n
i g n i s

—

Flesh is to spirit
as rubber is to lightning
(absorbing it)
as water is to lightning
(conducting it)

as wood is to fire
(feeding it)
as fire is to wood
(consuming it)

—

These are the flames that close around Dido

these are the waves slapping the ship's hull

this is the veil of flame passing over her face

and this is the veil revealing her face

—

Breughel remembered the men
who hewed the stone for Babel.
Infinite stone. A heaven of stone.
But in the Bible it was brick.
Brick requires not men but fire.

—

You move, the fire moves.

RADIO

A high rain

Hermes child

blazed heaves

of static, seized

with seraphsong

Now I know

I am nomad

M. DIDEROT YOU FORGET

Catherine the Great said
that I work in flesh and blood
while you work on paper
which will tolerate anything.

METAMORPHOSIS

Swiftly my human form galloped
away, and left me a horse.

FAMOUS LOCKS OF HAIR SPEAK

after Catullus 66

LEE HARVEY OSWALD

Even I don't know
whether he did it,
and whether alone.

He didn't sweat
in the interrogation
room;

his eyes looked
dead into America's

The shutter clicked.

MARILYN

I know what it's like
to be bleached almost white,
to suffer into beauty.

After the screen absorbed
every image, it glowed
a searing glow.

JFK

I was tangled and dripping water,
dripping blood and chemicals
on the autopsy table,
I was matted in the wound
the kill shot made.

Eros and Thanatos
were everything about him.
And a flame for a grave.

◆ PHOSPHORESCENT FICTION ◆

Sing this into the man's mouth. And both his ears.
Sing this into the wound. Then apply the salve.

—Nine Herbs Charm

It makes sense
it would be here
we would meet,

this being the only
intersection
in the world.

Summit speaks to summit,
slope to opposite slope.

Water speaks to water,
wind speaks
only to wind.

The heat of the sun speaks
to the heat of the sun.

But isn't it you, there, I speak to?

From all over Europe they come to settle
in this most glorious, most civilized city.

God came from Odessa to these great gates,
walked across this great courtyard, toward

the house of blond stone: God's bastard style
ran through its cunning corridors.

O it does still: day and night, through the seasons,
wood and gilt and marble break into ornament

under your gaze, enthralled, full of love, into torment.

When all are turned to bread,
who will break me?

When all are turned to stone,
who will quarry and carve me?

When all are turned to planets,
whose swirling dust will embrace me?

When all are turned to oceans,
on whose shore will I lie down?

When all are turned to light,
on what will I fall
and shatter into color?

When all the light goes dark,
who will get lost in me?

Who will parse the constellations
I reveal? Whose secrets will I hide?
And who will enter me for the last time?

There is complete silence
and there is the silence
you must complete

lay your own
lifetime of silence
carefully on the heap

which grows higher
and the lessness more resonant
each generation

there is no end to it
save in the frail moral sense
of the people

eventually we'll have enough
silence to call complete
and only then catch the omen

of the lethal genius of things
driving this world to its limits
on the wind

NINE POEMS

As if our souls had *asked* for frailty, pain, impermanence, and limitation.

The tunes lost all their notes. And became thoughts.

Not otherworldly. Unworldly.

As the topography rises out of the earth.

And the via negativa is also a forking path.

The poem as flypaper. Whatever lands on it, sticks.

The ratio of *history* to magic.

Clarities reestablish, where the traffic of dream images wore away, the threshold.

Vultures, as if they knew the truth about themselves, stagger around the carcass, too full to fly.

ONE OF THE THIRTY

I was struck
at Antioch
and wear
Alexander's face
on my own
face. On
my other
face, Fortune
holds a palm
branch, and a river
god no one worships
anymore
swims
at her feet.

For years I knit
the world
together; I
moved
one way and some
commodity
moved, like
the script of the
Hebrews, the
other. Roads were
built, and
cities; fortunes,
villas.
Cosmopolitan
life, prostitution,

charity
for the poor
and crazy—
all that I made.

Everybody wanted
me. I was
the bride at
every wedding,
and dowry for
more than
a few. Solid
and liquid
at once, my
silver body—
so many hands
touched.

Once I was used
to pay a bribe
and ended up
in a chest
of fragrant
cedar—
a secret
slush fund
only the provincial
governor
and his cronies
could access.
Am I responsible
for what a weak
man did

for the sake
of having me?
When it was
all over, he
threw me
and the others
at the petty tyrant's
feet. Money

can do
and undo; it
can go
back. In
a hundred
ages,—you cannot.

The atrocious desire—
do I awaken
it? Or merely
('merely')
give it
purpose?
It is not
my desire.
Fortune
holds a palm
branch. But
when I was
pressed
in Judas'
hand—you
would recognize it—
I shuddered.

Like God's unreality
traveling through
an unreal world,

you create something,

a phosphorescent friction
of a metaphysical character.

Granite, bronze . . . perhaps tablets of styrofoam would be my surest bet to reach you. Black marker on white styrofoam. To write the name of God.

Pagans! Our brute human want, our excess, our sick rituals, our palaces built on atrocity.

A voice of granite for granite and a voice of flesh for flesh. The translator thinks not.

KINGS

The good king sits in Dumferlin town
eating leviathan steaks.
What he is is what he makes.

The mouse king killed the python,
its black blood soaked the thatch.
The earth absorbed even that.

The young king killed the python,
and its black blood dried in the sun.
God's will be done.

The modern king built his house
to look like it grew straight out of the ground.
A burial mound.

The Ararat king got out and stretched his legs,
squinted into the new light, nothing to declare.
Choked on the new air.

The green king had a parrot and the parrot had a problem,
couldn't tell a person from a thing.
All day it made the sound of the telephone ring.

People loved the blue-eyed king,
his thoughts were clear as glass.
He was always the smartest boy in the class.

The king met a genie and told him,
make me healthy, wealthy and wise.
It just stared back at him through its genie eyes.

The boy king sucks a lollipop,
cherishing sour joy.
But something sucked his joy away.

The scholar king pushed his glasses
up his nose, and leveled his gaze.
Then wound his way back through the maze.

The copper king sighed.
Dark mountain's gone black.
The thief is on the rack.

The urn king asked his niece,
does it smash or does it shatter?
Does it matter?

The dying king gazed for long periods
at the shifting colors of paradise,
the swimming myriads.

King Cowboy wiped his mouth,
lit his lamp, sat down and wrote:
The road goes on forever, but I don't.

The barnyard king had a parrot,
it was screeching *mi ritrovai! mi ritrovai!*
Then he turned over in his sty.

The dumb king was nervous,
he was tight as a violin string.
Who can say what tomorrow's gonna bring?

THAT'S LIFE

Integers go all the way to infinity.

And the odd ones,
and the even, infinities half the size.

And all the real numbers,
an infinity of infinities,
sphere within sphere
within sphere, and each,

as John Ashbery says,
fits its hollow perfectly.

We live,
grains of sand, between the spheres.
Each of us occupies the no-space
between two of them.

And when they revolve in their places,
they grind us down, but we scratch
their inner and outer surfaces,
leaving wild zigzag scars,

and where the universe zigs, we zag, and that's life.

This is the lost

life   At this hour
what's lost in it
glows   Everything
glows

CREATION

Time emerges from a world without time . . .
—Carlo Rovelli

1

Everything emerges from what it is not.

A line comes from a point, a plane from a line.

Only dark things come to light.

Only the unforgivable can be forgiven.

Music comes from the earth, from the air.

Center comes from circumference
and circumference from center.

Geometry comes
from the human intellect.

2

Ancient times were different;
things emerged from what they were:

light came from light,
clay came from clay,
bread came from bread,

and God strode forth from God.

God strode forth
in a garden made from a garden
made from a garden *ad infinitum*.

And said it was good!

You say you are the last of your species? Another species
will come, a better one, made not from
the same clay, but from the same light.
                                        —Machado de Assis

The air forgave us
and took us up
in its fragrant body

The earth forgave us
and received us
as guests

The water forgave us
laved us
held us in its arms

The fire forgave us
its moral injury
who turned it loose
everywhere in the world
Dresden Hiroshima Nagasaki
Cambodia Laos
many other names

Then?

And then an angel came
and recombined the elements
haphazardly
and every part of us
was scattered in among them
And over the new world day broke

LIKE A BOOK

The wound is an opening in the body,
and the body is Being itself lying open
like a book.

ERRATA

Indeed, the capacity of light to carry
and convey information is perhaps its
most important characteristic, writes
Ian A. Walmsley in *Light: A Very Short
Introduction*. For light read Hermes.

—

In the beginning it was not the Word
but crazy gibberish broke the silence
that lay over the uncreated cosmos
according to the *Allogenes*, found at
Nag Hammadi in 1945: ZZAZZAZZA.

—

X always corresponds to y.
X never equals x.
'Because it was him; because it was me'—
no one ever wrote that.
You will never be at home in this life.

Monoliths in the open field.

—

Let the ashes speak.

Omphalos-foam.

—

Our village erupts.

The clown has a cloud for a heart.

I live on a houseboat made of clouds.

They mine for clouds in the rocky earth of the provinces.

The saint's teeth fit
in the palm of your hand.
Close your hand around them.
Then throw them into the sky.

EPITAPH

Now I know something
you don't.

◆ CLICK ◆

Or, there's Satan!
　　—Robert Browning,
　　　　"Soliloquy of the Spanish Cloister"

Look! It's spring! And you thought everything was dead!

Look! It's spring! Dew bedecks the eyelashes of the dead!
  And you thought everything was dead!

after Gunnar Ekelöf

SONG OF THE RIGHT-HAND MARGIN

Done that but first energy

Were literally events

The case I think to notice

July playing with typically doors

Gift honor flag the head

India ship they were on a fear way

Conditions were remember this being too short

If they for example the Suez dizzy

And see the Acropolis hand

With boat then the boat then the summertime

Between company sets and had that and was still setting

Fairly though ideas Paris years so in the end came for
whom

I liked Jerry right away

And on two and the others in the end to wait for the only
where songs look

Was and with headphones write an other

We're here even myself

By the by a regular practice

Generally opera the same reverse

The of hand first thereafter

Or yet happened reached all the now itself

Idea London we gathered so there was afternoon

She and family with a couch knew everything

The must make me

All up see anything

Happening in countered but in better

They really really Einstein

Have that care first that anyone started

I was I had and knew about Oedipus

Today in the windy godhead the first because

In that singing act

Into which I have would doesn't opens

Generally a new same

Was was seconds was the on was complete

Out there off the opening

We in this oversimplified light our never close began

And and from God known is between us are the work of
this hand

The work making many in the part added in the 90s

I want innovative suggestions

Wanted to launch a big movie history coincidence

The counter here one idea would be the Cathedral of St.
John of the Tracks

Where I can you can open it up for you

Then the in we are beginning

Making ladders here the just touch and in a hurry

Who hear sand probably gold

Watched the wooden stream

Night painting

Were a long time

To me the moment they were because he

With had been missed but actually were there

Come for a did it was a maybe

Tired and she did hot springs stars thinking

Environment might waver

Am I takes has to better or in my case unbelievable

Recall concertos written in but having zero as a road

Was dream enough but the seem alternative

Whom I celebrate if I happen to be there

Of an eye follows the real

To forget memories alone until 1988

Asked before the the but each no problem

Or the and poetry

Came dinner and the beautiful end of his getting

Some sort of coming to visit him poem

Was difficult before and I

English were there when I has gone

And everything in precedes somehow vivid

That I think so I only sit

All and the haircut shrinking

To no too home

During day and with everything ten-to-one

Had would look the way or both

Not more than I knew propaganda films

Invent God are arm the the that distance

Most of it a mirror of it

Well by the well-known

Than the since I included in a real eternal truth

The has a music play it

Steady gave was you very records many jazz but unknown

Master the raw kind of I heard

In everything street

For a year Beethoven footsteps were so far apart

See if but I get to be careful

The long at the restaurant

In the very fact that we were all on the new

Of each other which effort was put into

The room yet no instruction had risen

In that among Baltimore this most completed first

About other going wasn't back to having fun

Said it was fun but took us and I running through the
dawn

Language where I got costumes and reasoning

Restoration spectacular composition no that holds

Inside quicksand complicated monsters

Watch the fool into muckle logic

Content told him very far away

Behind the arras the American ago

Trade or craft for word was a mystery

Was going to was going it took it did take time

Already and again and then once only

O sand god

Wherever you go
is Mt Sinai;
for you are the place
of encounter.

God will meet you
in you, in the place
(the summit, most barren)
where earth meets air.

This is the diary of one who vanished
and whose absence took on human form.
But only after all other options had been exhausted.

PEOPLE DRAG THINGS

All over the earth,
people drag things
this way, and that way.
Heavy things.

They leave ruts
in the earth
behind them, they
fill with water
or do not.
White water.

Like comets, like sperm, like maggots,
they crawl across the earth,
people and their burdens,
going somewhere, going
nowhere.
Going.

Some alone, some
in twos and threes,
they pull
with all the strength
their bodies possess.
Their bodies.

Mountains
have not yet risen, rivers
have not yet been carved.
Or else they've already been leveled,
already run dry.

They do not have mornings yet,
or they have ceased having them,
they do not experience
the sloughing off of sleep,
they do not meet
the day in another's eyes.

They do not feel summer come full
as shadows gather under them
at noon, they do not
enter autumn's clarity, its
readiness, they do not feel it
as they drag their burdens
behind them.

Who meets the dead?
Only the dead.
Who meets
the eyes of the dead?

There is a word before speech,
or a word beyond speech,
on each
of their tongues.
The dead—
their tongues.

People drag things
this way and that,
over the earth,
over the earth.
The earth.

People drag things
this way and that,
leaving ruts in the earth
behind them, like
comets, like sperm,
like maggots, like apostrophes,
in twos, and threes,
a word on each
of their tongues,
all over the earth.
The earth.

JOHN WAYNE

Even you were born, John Wayne, even you.

To you water of the other world clung,
its amniotic stink held your body,
utterly crushable.

But Jocasta didn't leave you on a mountainside,
Jochebed didn't hide you in the rushes;

you were born,
in Iowa, named Marion Morrison, and grew.

You played football for USC,
and sat with Wyatt Earp.
You took off your hat and spat.
Blew up the Alamo
with a spear in your heart.
Won an Oscar, and died of cancer.

Even you were born, John Wayne, even you.

HISTORY

The god of the fish swam away
inaugurating the Piscine Enlightenment,
age of anxiety and revolutions,
and became the god of the rats.

The age passed and the god of the rats abdicated,
leaving the rodent multitude to wonder
whether all was now permitted,
and assumed the throne of the wasps.

The almighty god of the wasps sought asylum
among the bats, among the shrews,
but they turned him away.
Only the pigs would take him,
would take him in,
would take him as their god.

Oink oink said the bright spiritual light
wrapped in cloud
the god of the pigs was,
oink oink let there be,
oink oink thou shalt not.

The god of the pigs withdrew
into the abyss of his power.
There was a great cosmic suck
as air tried to fill the emptiness in itself
in the god's vacant sty.

And the god of the pigs migrated,

and went among the worms,
who had up to that point
lived in godless muddy bliss,
and they made him the great glowworm,
and he lodged in the place
where vision stops.

An age took
an age to pass.
And when it did,

the god of the worms absconded,
and at that moment the heavens opened
in several places at once, manna
fell
into their lumbricine element,
vast continents of it
for the throngs to feed on,

and it kept happening, and happens
still, and somewhere
far above them,
creatures undreamt of destroy each other
on a plain outside their city,

and the worm god is lost.

TEAMWORK

So many dead
such little creatures,
the worms

This is the fault
where my dead half falls
on its counterpart,
this is the rift
where my dead
half fits

                its twin;
this is the border
my dead half trespasses into life,
and back again.
This is the fissure
my attention guards, my in-
tention grinds, this
is the meeting-place,
living in death, dying in life,
one touching one,

                    this is the doing
and the coming undone,
the fugitive self, its *as if*
through its *if not* run
as through a needle's eye

It is only life and it is your
only life. This is the hush
out of and back into which it
comes and goes

My belatedness becomes me!

A butterfly is not a tiger.

CATHOLIC SCHOOL

The plastic clock
next to the crucifix
(wooden cross, tin
Christ) next
to the hand sanitizer dispenser,
next to the circuit breaker panel,
taps the seconds out.

Or: the plastic clock's
pulse muffles, each second,
the universe's hard, unending click.

A STILL LIFE

Chardin, The Frick

1

Objects: knots
in the continuity
of matter, a little life
clings to. Your eye may

> linger
> on may
> come to
> cling to.

2

Riddles, the
answers to which are
plums glass wine
water squash
wicker and stone.
The eye's flights
and perchings
in among them, its
waggle dance, its
drift and glide reveal
the tempers, the
timbres of stillness.

3

The glass of water. As if
an Ariel had slipped a
spangle of transparency
into the world's coarseness
for his own delight, or
for his tired old master's.

4

But it is all so much more intimate than that,
more fleshly, denser.
You could touch these things,
rearrange them if you chose.
The light is not beautiful without them.
They bear the marks of human use.
It is late. It is Prospero's world.

5

A world of particularity.
You can meditate on any of it.
It is a world of habit.
The same wine in the same container
is moved slightly from where it was
at this time yesterday, or left
in the same place untouched,
and come upon slightly later.

6

Time passes. It passes
in each thing, sugar,
wood, wicker, glass; it
passes over their
surfaces. Fills the house.

7

So the still life arrests us
and suspends us in our wanting
to touch, love, and perhaps explain.

Something in us leaves us
and travels outward, sourceward,
close to the heart of things,

with you, Chardin, our guide.
And as in all the stories
the guide falls away

and leaves us alone, the death
still wet on our hands and arms.
And then it too is gone.

AFTER POLIZIANO

You sent me wine;
now send me thirst.

FROM VASARI

Summoned by Sforza to Milan
who loved the lyre, Leonardo
made him a silver lyre
in the form of a horse skull.

FROM THE GONCOURT JOURNALS

George Sand whispered
into Flaubert's ear:
you're the only person here
who doesn't frighten me.

—

She shed a tear
over a poem
by Hugo, just
at the most sentimental
point.

—

her delicate hands hidden
almost entirely
in lace

TO MORANDI

To set matter free of its forms.
—But you, Morandi: you free matter
in its forms.

Not motion in stillness,
not stillness in stillness the eye perceives
as counter-motion, not
the breath of life hanging around
in the *nature morte* like the holy spirit
gathering over the face of the deep—

but freedom.
In your domestic constellations
of vases and bottles, in your light
grown worn with so much looking,
in your living

silence, you show us
this freedom: a freedom
different from the freedom of choice!

A freedom different from power.

When you died,
a thick coat of dust covered everything
in your studio. Not even the light disturbed it.

READING *SANDOVER*

Mirth, metaphysical
fizz, bat-and-
peacock-cackle
sounds down a long,
beautiful hall.

—

One could have been
the Son of Sam, you
mused. Instead
it was a long, safe,
blessèd journey.

ON IDEAS OF SCALE

That the nucleus occupies less
of the atom than I do
of the human species
is the purest kind of knowledge;
the body cannot grasp it.

It does not work its way
up through dumb muscle
into the viscera, does not,
there at the bottom of the edifice
the person is, I mean at
the heart, take hold.

I should like, one day,
to be turned to crystal,
my every atom knocked
into line, rank on rank
at attention, all of me
suddenly, sleek and abstract.

I would cloud the light
that entered me
slightly, then send it on its way.

I would have edges.

after Valerio Magrelli

GUEST

It came into his head and mind to go hunting,
he was minded to go hunting, Lady Guest translates.
There is another world
and it is not different from this one:
rather, this world is the space
the creatures of the other world inhabit.
They have something red on them. So he let loose his dogs
in the wound and sounded his horn (Lady Guest).
And whilst he listened to his hounds, he heard
the cry of other hounds, different
from his own. Let loose his dogs in the wood,
I meant to write. Let his dogs loose
in the wood and sounded his horn.

Pearls strung on a vector of force,

and each a burning Troy
from which, with everything

that to you is precious

in your arms, you flee.

Death differs from life only in one respect.
Otherwise the one fits the hollow of the other
almost perfectly.

See?
Everything clicks into place.
Their surfaces touch
at every point.
Look into your father's eyes.

◆ ORIGIN PIT ◆

"Ask you something? When it happened? The Day Everything Changed, where were you?"
"In my little cubicle. Reading Tacitus."

—Thomas Pynchon, *Bleeding Edge*

FESTIVAL OF THE SKELETONS

One day a year, after the harvest
comes in, they don
fleshsuits and
ape life.

God smashed the Logos to powder
and hid a speck in every living thing.

Now this lateness, these cruel colors . . .

Into the ear of the end, sing.

AGAINST A BACKGROUND OF SLOW QUIET STRINGS REPRESENTING THE SILENCE OF THE DRUIDS WHO KNOW SEE AND HEAR NOTHING

All praise to the Eurasian walnut (*Juglans regia*) with its large edible nuts and richly figured wood! And to the vast green tennis courts where it grows! And to the sparkling liquid that descends from clouds that ruins weddings but keeps everything green! And the many lawns that get parched in its place and die so they can live! And to those who own the lawns full of dust! And to those who mow the dust! Yeah!

THE NEWS FROM GRACELAND

Elvis's racquetball court has been restored to its 1977 condition. Elvis remains in his 1977 condition. America wants to be restored to its 1977 condition, being in the minds of many in Elvis's 1977 condition currently, in no shape, certainly, to be out on the racquetball court, certainly not being in Elvis's racquetball court's present condition, having recently been restored to its 1977 condition. For for the racquetball court to be restored to its 1977 condition is the opposite of for Elvis to remain in his 1977 condition, even though they happen at the same time and in the same place, namely in 1977 and in the present and in America.

The king is dead. Long live the king.

THE HUMAN REMAINS

to be seen.
The gods do not exist
for your sake.

—

History is written by the victors
in the nervous systems of the vanquished.

—

Why did Actaeon see Diana bathing?
Because his eyes were open.

The dogs tore him to pieces anyway.

His own dogs!

Your words are no truer for having been uttered in pain.

OPERATION DEADLIGHT

Scuttling the U-Boats, they tow
a hundred sixteen of them about
a hundred miles northwest of Ireland
in late 1945 and early '46.

Area XX is the main scuttling area,
though dozens of the boats   *Your hate—where do you put it?*
surrendered by the *Kriegsmarine*
were taken to YY and ZZ
for target practice by the Royal Navy
and Air Force.

The boats were to be sunk
using explosive charges,   *that which cannot be tolerated*
but due to storms   *as part of Earth's ecology*
most had to be destroyed
by naval guns.

You can see it on film—   *What kind of film?*
when one is hit, a sheet
of water leaps skyward
in the manner of the fountains
at the Bellagio in Las Vegas.

Some U-Boats were claimed as prizes   *Well, you have to put it somewhere—*
by Britain, France, Norway,
Russia, and even Japan.

In the late-1990s, a firm applied
for salvage rights to the Deadlight U-boats,
planning to raise up to a hundred of them.

Because the U-boats were constructed
in the pre-atomic age, the wrecks contain
metals that are not radioactively tainted,
and are therefore valuable to researchers.

Pasternak: I am a monster

RADIANT GIST

I scratched an itch
on my upper arm
It was a firefly
A little smear
a molten
glow going out

DREAM

If radiance could think
would it not think you,
my dear, would it not
think you into being
each night, and each morning
would it not think you out.

AMERICANARAMA

Within every bowling alley another,
fiercer bowling alley is trying to get out.

Every container ship
contains another, more heated
container ship.

Inside every cherry pie
a more developed cherry pie
waits for its fifteen minutes.

Concealed within the husk
of every electric guitar:
an electric guitar with greater
spiritual power.

At the heart of every AAA battery,
a more talented AAA battery lies dormant.

Within every apple,
an apple with a higher SAT score
awaits its moment in the sun.

Every hedge fund
is choking a bigger hedge fund to death
inside it.

Pity the reed cut
from the reed bed,
the hair clipped
from the queen's head.

Pity the wood
that finds itself
a violin. Pity the fox
and the hedgehog
and the teller of the tale.

Pity Coma Berenices
ashimmer in the astral
milk, Conon the astronomer pity,
in whose eyes.

Pity the prince
and his hot-blooded armada.

Pity the oxblood
dumped in the earth
and the ox that died
on my tongue. Pierrot
Le Fou pity, and pity
the waves of traffic
washing the street.

Catullus—pity even you.
Oh but pity us too.

THE *SCREEN TESTS*

something is concealed
almost successfully
in some faces
in others
not

THE END OF NATURE

After he burned the *Aeneid*, Virgil and his dog Meliboeus
went out walking. He walked to the end of Rome, then to
the end of the Empire, then he walked all the way to the end
of nature. The end of nature was a beach. He watched, high
above, a lone seagull drift, and glide . . . It was beautiful, the
moment at which the bird's drift folded into its glide. And in
time and space, so strict and unforgiving!

Albatross! barked Meliboeus.

The beach extended as far in either direction as Virgil could
see. He walked down it a long way. He'd already been to
Avernus—perhaps here would be another passage to another
world . . .

Perhaps there'd be another sybil inhabiting another cave.
Perhaps there'd be a sibyl so different from the one at Cumae
that he would not recognize her as a sibyl. Perhaps she'd
be living elsewhere than in a cave, or in a cave he did not
recognize as a cave—something totally different, a totally
different configuration of matter.

(But in the heart of the new sibyl, would it be the same god
that stirred?)

He walked along the beach as the sun hovered closer and
closer. Meliboeus trotted ahead, nosing his way, on the scent
of something, or nothing. Soon the sun would go down and
they would fall in shadow. What then?

Virgil stopped. He had walked very far. Centuries—millennia. His grand book was so much ash in a faraway hearth. He didn't care! The thought of his dramatic gesture grew dim in his mind. The world in which it had meaning was not this world!

Meliboeus looked into his eyes. Had he caught the scent of anything?

Man and dog lay down on some moss to sleep. Tomorrow perhaps they would try to find the way down. The only alternatives would be to go back to Rome, or to live there at the end of nature till the end of time. But Rome was long gone by now.

But as the sun set on the beach and sleep's tide rose, Virgil saw that there would be no thrill of passage, no dread sibyl, no threshold, no underworld journey, no transformation of values, no new language to learn, no law—there would be no burning city, no magic, no epic, no empire, no decline and fall—just Virgil and Meliboeus, poet and dog, darker and darker, there at the end, there at the end.

THE OPENING OF THE FIELD

I can see clear
to the horizon.
Everything is Illinois:
green and good!

Once, muddy giants
studded the earth.
They stood kneehigh
in the summer cornfields
of Illinois. So they
say. So many they
choked the vista. Something
must have happened to them.

What were they?
Did God grow them out of Illinois,
or did they come from somewhere else?

You thought they were angels
    from some sparkly somewhere,
or cast out of some
    sparkly somewhere,
but they were not—they were guardians,
    the guardians of Illinois!

Did they just disappear?

Do their giant bones sing in the sun and earth?

Could you hear them
if they were?   I can see

    clear to the horizon.

POEM

A thing becomes redeemable
only when you have lost everything.

Only dust is redeemable.

Will I cross
the threshold?

Where
will I be
then?

Does
that place
permit hope?

Afford
comfort?

Can you
breathe
there?

LAST MAN STANDING

Eventually someone will have to be the last,
Eventually it will come to that, whether
Because of or in spite of what we
                            will have by then done,
And will it matter
To that person, and what will be the
Pitch of his grief, and how will he mourn
Alone and toward what resolution
                            what forgiveness
With the poison
                knowledge he holds? I see
That person; I fill in the blanks. There are many
Blanks. Yes it is me, yes it is me
Of all the others it is me, he says, chuckling in disbelief.

Why should he disbelieve?
He is the priest of the end. He is the host

Of the end thriving in him as it
Thrived in all his bloodline,
And will not take no for an answer,

And he carries it,
And he carries it nowhere, nowhere at all.

What was, for a time, was good.
What was was good, for a time.
What was was, for a time, not
terrible. It was bearable. It was
able to be suffered, and to be
suffered through. We suffered,
sometimes, through it. What was
was what we sometimes called
good in spite of everything,
which is what it was: everything.
And it was good. And we suffered.

SUFFERING

Orpheus sings
not out of loss

but out of pain;
the unthinkable

is still unthinkable
even as it happens.

—

Even as it happens,
Orpheus sings.

It's still unthinkable.
Not out of loss,

the unthinkable,
but out of pain.

—

But out of pain,
even as it happens—

the unthinkable—
Orpheus sings.

Not *our* loss
is unthinkable.

—

It's still unthinkable.
But out of pain,

not out of loss,
even as it happens,

Orpheus sings
the unthinkable.

—

The unthinkable
is still unthinkable.

Orpheus sings,
but out of pain.

Even as it happens,
not out of loss.

—

Not out of loss.
The unthinkable—

even as it happens—
is still unthinkable.

But out of pain,
Orpheus sings.

RAIN

Rain is my native tongue I grew up speaking rain
learned to read rain fell in love in rain and even now
even here at the end of everything rain tints
and timbres my talk so much I forget almost
I forget no rain will ever fall on this place again

The prophets say
all is to be
other than it is.

Art will be short and life long.

Rivers will allow
repeat entry.

Age will be easy
and youth full of pain.

Plus
will repel
minus.

The scholar
will work by daylight
and subtract knowledge from the text
until it is reduced
to a field of luminous glyphs,

while his commentary will spawn commentary
in ever-smaller sections
that vanish in the center of the page.

Salt will salve
and ointment burn.

Wounds will heal in reverse.

The meek will inherit the earth.

The prophets
will not speak.

NOTES AND ACKNOWLEDGMENTS

Powers of the Earth
The phrase in quotes is from Eugenio Montale.

Against a Background of Slow Quiet Strings . . .
The title is from Charles Ives's *The Unanswered Question.*

Some of the poems in this book appeared in *New* and
Blazing Stadium. My gratitude to the editors.

"The void was too full of meaning" appeared in *The Wren
The Mind Allows To Sing,* edited by Billie Chernicoff.

Thanks to Brendan White for his help with these poems.

ABOUT THE AUTHOR

STEPHEN WILLIAMS is the author of *Earth Enough* (Dos Madres, 2021), *The Star of the End* (Dos Madres, 2022), and *Is and Isn't* (selva oscura, forthcoming 2026). He lives in Chicago.

Other books by Stephen Williams
published by Dos Madres Press

Earth Enough (2021)
The Star of the End (2022)

For the full Dos Madres Press catalog:
www.dosmadres.com